Ethan Claymore

D1565189

Also by Norm Foster:

Ethan Claymore

by
Norm Foster

Playwrights Canada Press
Toronto

Playwrights Canada Press
269 Richmond St. W., Suite 202, Toronto, ON M5V 1X1
416.703.0013 • info@playwrightscanada.com
www.playwrightscanada.com

Playwrights Canada Press acknowledges the financial support of the
Government of Canada through the Canada Book Fund and the Canada
Council for the Arts, and of the Province of Ontario through the Ontario
Arts Council and the Ontario Media Development Corporation for our
publishing activities.

Cover design by JLArt

Library and Archives Canada Cataloguing in Publication
Foster, Norm, 1949–
    Ethan Claymore

A play.
ISBN 978-0-88754-581-8

I. Title.

PS8561.O7745E83 2000   C812'.54   C99-932578-7
PR9199.3.F67E83 2000

First edition: 2000
Second printing: August 2012
Printed and bound in Canada by Marquis Book Printing, Montreal

Dedication

For my children
Lee, Randy, Daniel & Jacqueline

Ethan Claymore was first produced at The Grand Theatre in London Ontario, October 30–November 13, 1998.

ETHAN CLAYMORE	Ric Reid
MARTIN CLAYMORE	David Ferry
DOUGLAS MCLAREN	Jerry Franken
TERESA PIKE	Catherine Fitch
YOUNG ETHAN	Scott Wilkinson
YOUNG MARTIN	Nik Longstaff

Directed by Miles Potter
Set & Costumes by Peter Hartwell
Lighting Design by Erica Hassell
Stage Manager: Lauren Snell
Assistant Stage Manager: A. Naomi Wiebe

CHARACTERS

ETHAN CLAYMORE	38 years old
MARTIN CLAYMORE	43 years old
DOUGLAS MCLAREN	In his fifties or sixties
TERESA PIKE	In her thirties
YOUNG ETHAN	12 years old
YOUNG MARTIN	16 years old

ACT ONE

Scene One

TIME: The present. Monday, December 21st.
PLACE: The home of Ethan Claymore.

> *It is a farmhouse. The kitchen and the living areas are contained in the same space. There is a kitchen table and chairs in the room and a woodstove for heat. There is also an easel in the room on which sits a canvas, and there is a small table with paints nearby. There is a door leading outside, and a window, which looks out into the front yard.*
>
> *As the lights come up there is no one onstage. It is night. The room is dark. We see a figure pass by the window. It is DOUGLAS MCLAREN, a man in his fifties. He wears a winter coat over his overalls. He knocks on the door.*

DOUGLAS   *(off)* Ethan!!? Ethan!! *(He knocks again.)* It's December the twenty-first, now open up!! *(He cups his hands around his eyes and peers in through the window.)* I know you're in there, Ethan, now open this door before I break it down!!

> *ETHAN CLAYMORE enters from his bedroom. He is tying a robe around himself as he moves.*

ETHAN   What the.... Who's there?

DOUGLAS   Never mind who's here. Just open this door!

ETHAN	Douglas? *(He moves to the door and opens it.)* Douglas, what are you doing?

DOUGLAS marches into the room.

DOUGLAS	Ethan, it's December the twenty-first.
ETHAN	What?
DOUGLAS	It's December the twenty-first.
ETHAN	December the twenty-first.
DOUGLAS	Yes.
ETHAN	Well, thank you, Douglas. Are you spreading this news to all the neighbours, or just the ones you suspect of being without calendars?
DOUGLAS	Ethan, I've come to inform you that your period of mourning is officially over.
ETHAN	My what?
DOUGLAS	December the twentieth, five years ago, your Jenny passed on, rest her soul.
ETHAN	Yes. And?
DOUGLAS	And you've been mourning that sweet thing for five years now. Well, it's over, Ethan. Enough is enough. For five years I've watched you work this place all by yourself, never visiting your neighbours, never attending any social functions, never going out *at all* for that matter. Not to mention the fact that you haven't celebrated Christmas for five years. Good heavens, Ethan, you don't even put up a Christmas tree any-

more. Well, it's December the twenty-first, and that is going to change starting today. Starting right now!

ETHAN   Douglas, it's one a.m...

DOUGLAS   Yes, it is. And it's over. Today, you are returning to the world of the living. And I'm the one who is going to lead you there.

ETHAN   You?

DOUGLAS   Me. Douglas Aloysius McLaren. Now, I've taken the liberty of drawing up a list of things we have to do. *(He takes a piece of paper out of his pocket.)*

ETHAN   Douglas...

DOUGLAS   Uh-uh-uh!! You just hold your tongue until I'm through. Now, sit down. Sit, sit.

ETHAN sits.

All right, now. Number one. We're going to get you some new clothes. I am sick and tired of seeing you in those godforsaken overalls of yours. How do you expect to make an impression when you walk around looking like Little Abner every day?

ETHAN   What about you? You wear overalls.

DOUGLAS   I'm married. I don't have to impress anyone.

ETHAN   And who do I have to impress?

DOUGLAS   Teresa Pike. Number two on my list. I'm going to introduce you to her.

ETHAN   Who?

DOUGLAS   Teresa Pike. She moved to Gladden's Head four months ago. She's a teacher at the public school.

ETHAN   Never heard of her.

DOUGLAS   Well, of course you haven't, you donkey's ass. You never go out. You never talk to anyone. How would you hear anything!?

ETHAN   Donkey's ass? Isn't that redundant?

DOUGLAS   Never mind! You're going to meet her and you're going to like her!

ETHAN   Douglas, I don't want to meet...

DOUGLAS   Uh-uh-uh!! It's been decided. There's no point in arguing. That brings me to number three. You work too much, Ethan. You need to consort more. Fraternize. And to that end, you're going to start coming with me to Robert Ludlow's Fina Station, and you're going to sit around there and talk to me and Robert and Woody Hull and Calvin Chase.

ETHAN   What'll we talk about?

DOUGLAS   Nothing. Not a blessed thing. That's the whole point. That's why I go there every afternoon.

ETHAN   So you can talk to Robert, and Woody...

DOUGLAS   And Calvin, yes.

ETHAN   About nothing.

DOUGLAS   Absolutely nothing. The afternoon
                passes and our minds go completely
                unchallenged.

ETHAN   And you enjoy this?

DOUGLAS   I wouldn't miss it for the world. And
                you'll feel the same way, I guarantee it.
                (looking at his list) And finally, number
                four. A Christmas tree. Something to
                brighten up this tomb you've buried
                yourself in. You leave that one up to
                me. I won't rest until I find you the
                perfect Christmas tree, Ethan. A tree
                that'll fire up the Christmas spirit, and
                set you on the road to recovery. There.
                That's it. That's the list. You can go
                back to sleep now. *(He puts his list
                away.)*

ETHAN   Have you been drinking, Douglas?

DOUGLAS   I had an eggnog.

ETHAN   Did you put anything in it?

DOUGLAS   Half a pint of rum if it's any of your
                business! Now, you march yourself
                into that bedroom of yours and get
                some sleep, Ethan Claymore, because
                you've got a big day ahead of you, and I
                want you at your best. Goodnight, sir!
                (He exits.)

                *DOUGLAS walks by the window, glances
                in, and sees that ETHAN hasn't moved.*

                I said get to bed!

ETHAN   All right, I'm going.

                *ETHAN exits to the bedroom. Lights
                down.*

ACT ONE

Scene Two

TIME: That same morning. Monday, December 21st.
PLACE: The same.

> *Lights up, there is no one onstage.*
> *ETHAN enters through the door. He is*
> *wearing a winter coat over overalls now*
> *and he is carrying a small basket of eggs.*
> *He puts the basket in the refrigerator, and*
> *takes one egg with him to the stove. He*
> *takes off his coat and hangs it up, then he*
> *takes out a frying pan and places it on the*
> *stove. DOUGLAS enters. He is*
> *carrying some mail. He stands there as if*
> *expecting ETHAN to say something.*
> *ETHAN turns around and sees him.*

ETHAN   Oh, good morning, Douglas.

DOUGLAS   I suppose you didn't see me out there.

ETHAN   Out where?

DOUGLAS   Walking up the road to your house
here.

ETHAN   Oh, were you walking up my road?

DOUGLAS   Yes, I was walking up your road.

ETHAN   Well, no, I guess I didn't see you.

DOUGLAS   And you didn't hear me call to you
either, I suppose.

ETHAN   Did you call to me?

DOUGLAS
Several times. "Morning Ethan!", I said. Then I said it again. *(He waves.)* "Morning Ethan! I got your mail for you!" You see that there? That's a wave. I was calling and waving.

ETHAN
Well, I'm sorry, Douglas. Someone disturbed my sleep last night and this morning my senses aren't as sharp as they could be.

ETHAN takes the mail from DOUGLAS.

DOUGLAS
You're welcome.

ETHAN
So, what can I do for you... Aloysius?

DOUGLAS
Oh, so, you remember my visit last night, do you?

ETHAN
Yes, I do. Do you?

DOUGLAS
Yes, quite vividly. And did you think about what I said?

ETHAN
Douglas, you had a snootfull last night, and you were babbling. Now, I'm willing to forget about it if you are. *(looking at the mail)* Look at these bills. This is the favour you do me? Bringing my bills in for me? Some friend. Final notice it says. Look at that.

DOUGLAS
Are you falling behind?

ETHAN
No, I started behind. I just haven't caught up yet.

DOUGLAS
What is it? Business not good?

ETHAN
Oh, it's about the same, Douglas. The problem is my expenses keep going up. And my truck died yesterday and now

I've got to get that fixed too. Would you like some breakfast?

DOUGLAS   No, we haven't got time for breakfast. We have to get over to Erdie's Men's Wear. They open in fifteen minutes.

ETHAN   Erdie's men's wear?

DOUGLAS   *(takes his list out of his pocket)* Number one on my list. New clothes.

ETHAN   Douglas, I am not getting any new clothes. I can't afford new clothes.

DOUGLAS   Well, how are you going to impress Teresa Pike looking like a... an egg farmer?

ETHAN   I am an egg farmer.

DOUGLAS   But, you don't have to look like one. I mean, look at me, I grow corn. Do I look like a corn grower?

ETHAN   No, you don't.

DOUGLAS   You see?

ETHAN   You look like an egg farmer. *(He opens a piece of mail.)*

DOUGLAS   Ethan, cut it out. Now, you're going to make an impression on this woman whether you like it or not.

ETHAN   No, I'm not, Douglas, because I won't even be meeting the woman. *(He starts to read the letter.)*

DOUGLAS   Well, that's where you're wrong, Ethan. You see here? Number two on my list. Introduce Ethan to Teresa Pike. Well, on my way over here this morning I stopped by the school and had a word with Miss Pike. I explained to her that it was a custom in this area for the new teachers to introduce themselves around to all the parents, and that it seems that everyone's met her except for this friend of mine named Ethan Claymore. Mind you, I didn't tell her that you weren't a parent, but that's a small point. Well, she was very apologetic and she promised that she'd stop by after school this afternoon and make your acquaintance. Now, I can be here to help break the ice if you like, but personally I think that my presence would be an intrusion, and Lord knows I've never been one to intrude.

ETHAN doesn't respond.

Ethan? Did you hear what I said?

ETHAN   *(not listening)* Uh... I'm sorry, Douglas, no I didn't.

DOUGLAS   Ethan, what's the matter?

ETHAN   Nothing. Uh.... It seems my brother's passed away.

DOUGLAS   Your brother?

ETHAN   Yes. Martin.

DOUGLAS   I didn't even know you had a brother. You've never spoken about a brother.

ETHAN   Well, he's been selling cars back home for the past... I don't know... fifteen years. It says he had a heart attack. Forty-three years old.

DOUGLAS   Ethan, I'm sorry.

ETHAN   No, that's okay. We weren't very... I mean, I haven't talked to him in a long time. *(He puts the letter away.)* Now, what were you saying?

DOUGLAS   Uh... nothing. It can wait.

ETHAN   Are you sure?

DOUGLAS   Yes, yes. Is there anything I can do, Ethan?

ETHAN   No.

DOUGLAS   I mean, Caroline and I, we're just down the road. If there's anything you need, just call us.

ETHAN   Douglas, I'm fine. Really.

DOUGLAS   Well, all right. I'd better go then.

ETHAN   You just got here.

DOUGLAS   I know, but I'd better go. I'll leave you to your thoughts.

ETHAN   You're not going to pester me about your list anymore?

DOUGLAS   Tomorrow. There'll be plenty of time for pestering tomorrow. For now, I'll just get out of your way.

ETHAN   Oh, Douglas, wait. *(He moves to the refrigerator and takes out the basket of eggs.)* Take these to Caroline, would you? She said she was going to make egg bread today. *(He gives the basket to DOUGLAS.)*

DOUGLAS Oh, certainly. Thank you. I'll see you tomorrow then. Goodbye, Ethan.

DOUGLAS exits. ETHAN picks up the letter. We flashback to ETHAN'S childhood. Two young boys, YOUNG MARTIN and YOUNG ETHAN enter from ETHAN'S bedroom. MARTIN is sixteen, ETHAN is eleven. MARTIN carries a pair of skates and a hockey stick.

YNG. ETHAN Come on, Martin, why can't I play too?

YNG. MARTIN Because you can't, Nancy. You can't even skate. You'll just get in the way.

YNG. ETHAN I can too skate.

YNG. MARTIN Not like us you can't.

YNG. ETHAN *(moving to ETHAN at the counter)* Dad, Martin won't let me play hockey with him.

ETHAN Well, he's right, Ethan. Those boys are big. You'll get in the way and you'll get hurt.

YNG. ETHAN Dad, please. I'll be careful.

ETHAN No, Ethan.

YNG. ETHAN Please. I'll just stay off to the side until somebody passes it to me. I'll stay away from everybody. Please.

ETHAN Ethan...

YNG. ETHAN Please?

ETHAN *(Beat.)* All right, just this once then.

YNG. ETHAN Yayyy! I'll get my stuff. *(He exits to the bedroom.)*

YNG. MARTIN   Aw, Dad, does he have to??

ETHAN   Just this once, Martin. As soon as he sees how hard it is to play with you fellas, he won't ask again. And you look out for him, you hear? Don't let the other boys knock him around any. I don't want him coming back here in tears. All right?

YNG. MARTIN   Yeah.

ETHAN   And don't stick him in goal either.

YNG. MARTIN   Yeah.

ETHAN   And after you've finished playing, I want you to work on your stops and starts. That scout's going to be at the game tomorrow and I want him to see what a good two-way player you are. Okay?

YNG. MARTIN   Yep.

ETHAN   Good boy.

YNG. MARTIN   I can't believe he's coming all the way from Toronto just to see me.

ETHAN   Well, he's an old friend of mine, and that's what friends do for each other. Family and friends, Martin. The two most important things in life. Remember that.

YNG. MARTIN   How could I forget? You say it every other day.

ETHAN   And for good reason. But, now, he's not gonna recommend you to a junior team just because he's a friend. You're going to have to impress him, all right?

YNG. MARTIN   I will.

YOUNG ETHAN enters from the bedroom carrying a pair of skates and a hockey stick.

YNG. ETHAN   Okay, I'm ready.

YNG. MARTIN   Come on then.

ETHAN   Martin? *(He grabs a banana from the counter and tosses it to YOUNG MARTIN.)* Here. You need your potassium for those young muscles.

YNG. MARTIN   Thanks, Dad.

YOUNG MARTIN exits.

ETHAN   Ethan? You be careful now.

YNG. ETHAN   I will.

ETHAN   And if they try to put you in goal, say no.

YNG. ETHAN   Okay. *(He starts for the door.)*

ETHAN   Oh, Ethan, have you finished the painting for your mother yet?

YNG. ETHAN   Not yet.

ETHAN   Well, you'd better get a move on. Christmas will be here before you know it.

YNG. ETHAN   I will.

YOUNG MARTIN enters again.

YNG. MARTIN   Come on, Nancy, let's go.

YOUNG MARTIN exits.

YNG. ETHAN   Dad, Martin called me Nancy again.

ETHAN   Just go, Ethan. Go on.

YNG. ETHAN   Goodbye, Dad. Wait up, Martin!! *(He exits.)*

Lights down.

ACT ONE

Scene Three

TIME: Later that afternoon
PLACE: The same.

Lights up to reveal ETHAN standing at his easel, painting. There is a knock on the door. ETHAN opens the door. TERESA PIKE is there. She is a woman in her thirties. She carries a bakery box, and an old briefcase.

TERESA   Mr. Claymore?

ETHAN   Yes.

TERESA   Hello. I'm Teresa Pike. I'm a teacher at the public school.

ETHAN   How do you do?

TERESA   Fine, thank you. I'm afraid I've been remiss in getting around to meeting you.

ETHAN   Meeting me?

TERESA   Yes. Do you have a moment?

ETHAN   Uh... sure. Come in.

TERESA   Thank you.

She enters.

I know I should have come here long before now, but I was unaware of the local custom. Oh, here. This is for you. *(She hands him the box.)* It's a cherry pie.

	I stopped off at Mrs. Bright's Bakery on my way.
ETHAN	*(takes the pie)* Thank you.
TERESA	I moved out here from the city, and in the city of course it would be difficult to get around and visit all of the parents, but with the smaller classes here, I guess it's more feasible.
ETHAN	The parents?
TERESA	Yes. And I quite like the idea actually. Getting around to the children's homes will give me a chance to see their environments. Now, I haven't met any Claymore children yet. I teach grades four and five. Yours must be in a lower grade, is that right?
ETHAN	My what? My children?
TERESA	*(notices the painting material)* Oh, someone in the family paints. That's nice. I think it's good for a child to be exposed to art. It provides a nice balance to the academic side of things. So, who's the artist? Your wife? You?
ETHAN	Uh... no Miss Pike, my wife died five years ago.
TERESA	Oh, I'm sorry. I didn't know.
ETHAN	No, that's all right.
TERESA	So, it's you then? You're the artist.
ETHAN	Hmm? Oh, yes, well, I try. Miss Pike, I think there's been a misunder...

TERESA   *(looking at the canvas)* Oh, that's very good. That's exceptional.

ETHAN   *(Beat.)* Really?

TERESA   Yes. It has heart. Depth. It's very reminiscent of Bierstadt's landscapes.

ETHAN   Bierstadt? You think so?

TERESA   Oh, yes.

ETHAN   I do like Bierstadt.

TERESA   Well, you can see the influence.

ETHAN   Did you study art?

TERESA   Books. I read books. I haven't got cable. Yes, that's very good indeed.

ETHAN   Thank you.

TERESA   So, how many children do you have?

ETHAN   *(looking at his painting)* None.

TERESA   None?

ETHAN   None. I was having trouble with the shading in the background, but it's starting to come around I think.

TERESA   I thought you had children.

ETHAN   Uh... no.

TERESA   Well... are they grown up? Moved away?

ETHAN   No. Never had any. Can I get you a cup of tea? It's already made.

TERESA	Uh.... Well, there's no point in my staying if you don't have children.
ETHAN	Oh.
TERESA	I thought you had children.
ETHAN	No.
TERESA	Because that's why I came. That's why I brought the pie.
ETHAN	My neighbours have children. I could call them over.
TERESA	No, no. That's fine.
ETHAN	They're nice kids. At least that's what I hear.
TERESA	No. Never mind.
ETHAN	So, will you have some tea?
TERESA	Uh... well... it's already made you say?
ETHAN	Yes.
TERESA	Well, as long as I'm here anyway, all right, then.
ETHAN	Good. *(He moves to get the tea.)*
TERESA	Why did I think you had children?
ETHAN	No idea.
TERESA	Would you like to have children?

There is a pause as ETHAN looks at TERESA.

I mean, someday. With someone.

ETHAN Well, if I was going to have children,
"with someone" would be a good way.

TERESA No, I was just thinking that if you were
going to have children, I would probably be their teacher one day, that's all.

ETHAN You plan to be here for a while then, do
you?

TERESA Well, I like it here, yes. It's away from
everything.

DOUGLAS bursts in the door.

DOUGLAS Ethan? *(He sees TERESA.)* Oh, Miss
Pike. You're here already.

TERESA *(to DOUGLAS)* You. You told me he
had children.

DOUGLAS No, I didn't. No, I said you should get
around to meet all the parents. And I
said my friend here hadn't met you yet.
You must've assumed from that some-
how, that he had children. *(to ETHAN)*
Ethan, I'm sorry, I forgot that I set this
up. And then when I remembered, I
rushed over as quickly as I could, but...
Miss Pike, I'm afraid you're going to
have to leave.

ETHAN Douglas, no...

DOUGLAS No, Ethan, it's all right. It's my mess.
I'll clean it up. Miss Pike, Ethan's just
suffered a loss in the family so this
might not be a good time.

TERESA *(to ETHAN)* I thought your wife died
five years ago.

DOUGLAS	No, not his wife. His brother. He just got word today.
TERESA	Oh, I'm sorry.
ETHAN	No, that's all right.
DOUGLAS	*(to TERESA)* So, if it's all right with you, maybe we can reschedule.
TERESA	Certainly. Reschedule what?
DOUGLAS	Your meeting.
ETHAN	Douglas, I was just going to pour some tea.
DOUGLAS	Oh, no thank you, Ethan. None for me. Miss Pike? I'll see you home.
ETHAN	Douglas, Miss Pike is staying for tea.
DOUGLAS	She is?
ETHAN	Yes.
DOUGLAS	Oh. *(Beat.)* Why?
ETHAN	Because I invited her to.
DOUGLAS	You did?
ETHAN	Yes.
DOUGLAS	Oh. Oh!! Well, then I've interrupted something. I'm sorry.
TERESA	No, we were just talking about having children.
DOUGLAS	*(Beat.)* Well, then there's no point in my staying around is there? I'd only be in the way. Well, I'll just run along then.

Sorry to barge in like that. Miss Pike, you have a nice day.

TERESA You too.

DOUGLAS Thank you. I will. Ethan.

ETHAN Goodbye, Douglas.

DOUGLAS exits and closes the door.

Have a seat, please.

TERESA Thank you. *(She moves to the table and sits.)*

The door opens and DOUGLAS enters again and speaks to TERESA.

DOUGLAS By the way, those are just his work clothes.

ETHAN Douglas?

DOUGLAS *(to TERESA)* I mean, when he puts his mind to it, he can slick up real nicely.

ETHAN Douglas...

DOUGLAS Goodbye now.

DOUGLAS exits.

ETHAN You'll have to excuse Douglas. He thinks he's helping me.

TERESA Helping you what?

ETHAN Well... get back into socializing I guess.

TERESA You haven't been socializing?

ETHAN Well, not according to Douglas I haven't

been. But, this farm keeps me pretty busy. I've got two thousand hens out there that I have to tend to, and I'm the only employee I've got so, there's not much time for anything else. And what extra time I do find, I spend right there at the easel.

TERESA   Uh-huh. So, your brother... he really died?

ETHAN   That's what it said in the letter.

TERESA   The reason I ask is that you don't seem terribly upset.

ETHAN   Well, Martin and I were very different. We didn't speak much. *(He moves down with the teapot and cups on a tray.)* Here we go. Just help yourself to the milk and sugar. *(He sets the tray down on the table.)*

TERESA   Thank you.

ETHAN   *(moves to his easel)* So it reminds you of Bierstadt, huh? That's interesting.

TERESA   Yes. Did you paint that from a photograph? There are certainly no mountains like that around here.

ETHAN   No, it's from memory. I grew up near the mountains.

TERESA   Oh.

ETHAN   I moved to Gladden's Head with my wife just after we got married.

TERESA   Why Gladden's Head?

ETHAN   Well, we just wanted to get away I

guess. Jenny was a sculptor and... well, we had this idea that we were going to live the idyllic artisan's life.

TERESA And did you?

ETHAN No, we found out, much to our surprise, that you have to have money to live, so we borrowed some and bought this egg farm.

TERESA How did your wife die, Mr. Claymore?

ETHAN Leukemia. And please, call me Ethan.

TERESA All right. Ethan.

ETHAN And enough about my life. What about you? What brings you to Gladden's Head?

TERESA The job.

ETHAN That's it?

TERESA That's it. You go where the work is.

ETHAN And where's home?

TERESA Ottawa. *(Awkward pause.)* The nation's capital.

ETHAN *(Beat.)* The parliament buildings are there.

TERESA That's the place. *(Beat.)* So, can you really slick up nicely?

ETHAN What? Oh! Well, I don't know. It's been so long since I slicked up for anything.

TERESA	Well, if you're looking for an excuse to, the school's having a parent's Christmas party Wednesday night. You could slick up and go to that.
ETHAN	But, I'm not a parent.
TERESA	Well, I could probably sneak you in.
ETHAN	But, Wednesday, that's the day after tomorrow.
TERESA	So?
ETHAN	*(looking at his clothes)* Well, it's just that I haven't got any... I mean, it's short notice.
TERESA	Well, it was just a thought.
ETHAN	Uh-huh. A party. I haven't been to a party in... I don't know how long.
TERESA	Five years?
ETHAN	About that.
TERESA	Well, if you're not busy that night, it should be fun. Rumour has it Paul Campbell's going to show us his appendicitis scar.
ETHAN	Well, that does sweeten the pot. Thanks. I'll think about it.
TERESA	Well, I'd better get going. I've got a lot of tests to mark tonight. *(She stands.)*
ETHAN	Oh, okay.
TERESA	Thank you very much for the tea.
ETHAN	You're welcome.

TERESA	And uh... well, maybe we'll see you at the party.
ETHAN	Well, I don't know about that, but, we'll see. *(He opens the door for her.)* And thanks for the pie, Miss Pike.
TERESA	Teresa.
ETHAN	Teresa. Good.
TERESA	Goodbye.
ETHAN	Bye now.

TERESA exits. ETHAN closes the door. He goes to his painting and looks at it. The door opens and DOUGLAS enters.

DOUGLAS	Well??
ETHAN	Douglas? Back so soon?
DOUGLAS	I never left. I was waiting in the chicken barn.
ETHAN	Waiting for what?
DOUGLAS	To see how it went. Now, how'd it go? Did you like her?
ETHAN	She's fine.
DOUGLAS	Fine? Just fine?
ETHAN	She's fine.
DOUGLAS	Well, what did you talk about, besides having children?
ETHAN	We weren't talking about having children. We were talking about children in general. We were making small talk.

I mean, she was only here a few minutes.

DOUGLAS   Oh. So, you didn't hit it off?

ETHAN   What do you mean, hit it off?

DOUGLAS   Well, sparks? Were there any sparks?

ETHAN   No, Douglas, there were no sparks.

DOUGLAS   Any smoke? Because you know, where there's smoke, there's fire.

ETHAN   No. No smoke. (*He picks up the tray of tea and moves it to the counter.*)

DOUGLAS: No heat of any kind?

ETHAN   No, Douglas.

DOUGLAS   Well, then you just weren't trying, Ethan. You just plain weren't trying. Darn it, how am I supposed to help you if you won't put forth the effort?

ETHAN   I don't know, Douglas.

DOUGLAS: Well, I'm not giving up. No sir. Douglas McLaren is no quitter. And you're about to find that out.

DOUGLAS opens the door and starts to leave.

ETHAN   Douglas?

DOUGLAS   (*stopping*) What?

ETHAN   What time does Erdie's Men's Wear stay open 'til tonight?

DOUGLAS   Erdie's? Six o'clock I think.

ETHAN	Thanks.
DOUGLAS	Why? Are you thinking of.... You're not thinking of...
ETHAN	I'm thinking about it.
DOUGLAS	Oh. Good. Well, if you can't make it by six, I could call Erdie and tell him to stay open a bit longer.
ETHAN	No, that's okay. I can make it.
DOUGLAS	Yessir!! One more thing I can cross off my list! Oh, I'm working on the Christmas tree, Ethan. I got a line on a good tree lot over in Vicker's Rock. I'll head over there tomorrow morning.
ETHAN	That's thirty miles away.
DOUGLAS	I told you, Ethan. I'm not buying just any tree. I'm buying you the perfect tree.
ETHAN	Well, you do what you like, Douglas, but I'm telling you, it won't get put to much use here.
DOUGLAS	Oh, we'll see about that. *(He starts to leave and then returns.)* Oh, by the way, Ethan, tomorrow afternoon we're going to the Fina station.
ETHAN	We're what?
DOUGLAS	Number three on my list. Remember?
ETHAN	Oh, right. Sit around and talk about nothing.
DOUGLAS	That's right.

ETHAN   Well, we'll see how busy I am. *(He has his back to DOUGLAS as he works at the counter.)*

                 MARTIN CLAYMORE enters through the open door. He is wearing a business suit. DOUGLAS cannot see him, and ETHAN isn't looking. MARTIN looks around the room, then wanders over to the easel and looks at the painting.

DOUGLAS   Never mind that. You're going. I've already told the boys you'll be there. They're very excited. New blood and all that. All right?

ETHAN   We'll see.

DOUGLAS   Good. I'll pick you up at two. So long, Ethan.

                 DOUGLAS exits and closes the door.

MARTIN   Still painting I see, Nancy.

ETHAN   *(turning around)* What? *(Beat.)* Oh, my God. Oh my God. Martin? Is that you?

MARTIN   Been a long time, Ethan.

ETHAN   Martin? I... I thought you were dead.

MARTIN   I am.

ETHAN   You are what?

MARTIN   Dead. Very much so.

ETHAN   No, I mean, I got a letter saying that you had died. It said you had a heart attack.

MARTIN   I did have a heart attack.

ETHAN   No, it said you died.

MARTIN   I did die.

ETHAN   No, it said you were dead.

MARTIN   I am dead. Exactly what part of this don't you understand?

ETHAN   I don't understand any of this.

MARTIN   All right, let me try and explain. Last week, I was showing a young couple this used Riviera on the car lot. The young lady—quite a striking woman—the young lady says to me can they take it for a test drive. And I says "Sure. Just let me go inside and get the..."

ETHAN   Get the what?

MARTIN   Nothing. That's as far as I got. Next thing I know I'm down on one knee and I'm hanging on to the Riviera's bumper. The young woman asks me if I'm all right, and I say, "I'll be fine." Those were my last words. "I'll be fine."

ETHAN   So, you *did* have a heart attack.

MARTIN   I sure did. Hurt like hell. I thought I was gonna die. Turns out I was right.

ETHAN   Wait a minute. What are you saying?

MARTIN   I'm trying to tell you that I'm dead, Ethan. And I'm not happy about it either. I could've sold that Riviera.

ETHAN   All right, Martin, what is this? What are you trying to pull?

> *The door opens and DOUGLAS enters again.*

DOUGLAS   Ethan, you'll want me to come with you to Erdie's, of course. I mean, I have a pretty keen eye for fashion as you can tell, so you'll probably want me to be there, right?

> *ETHAN doesn't answer.*

Ethan?

MARTIN   Hey, Douglas? Over here.

DOUGLAS   Ethan, are you going to answer me or not?

MARTIN   Douglas?? Yoo-hoo? *(He moves to the door.)*

DOUGLAS   Well, fine then. If you don't want me to come, just say so. You don't have to ignore me. *(He turns to leave.)*

ETHAN   Douglas?

DOUGLAS   What?

ETHAN   You can't see him?

DOUGLAS   See who?

ETHAN   Him. Right there.

DOUGLAS   Right where? *(looking around)*

ETHAN   Right there. There.

MARTIN   Forget it, Ethan. He'll think you're crazy.

DOUGLAS   What are you, crazy?

MARTIN	Too late.
DOUGLAS	Now, you call me when you're ready to go to Erdie's, all right? And have a nap. You're seeing things that aren't there.

DOUGLAS exits and closes the door.

ETHAN	He didn't see you.
MARTIN	That's right.
ETHAN	No, I mean, he didn't see you at all. Like you were invisible.
MARTIN	Now you're catching on.
ETHAN	Oh, now wait a minute, wait a minute, wait a minute.
MARTIN	It's true, Ethan.
ETHAN	No, it's not.
MARTIN	I know it's a shock, but it's true.
ETHAN	You're a ghost?
MARTIN	No, they don't call us ghosts. We're shadow beings.
ETHAN	Shadow beings?
MARTIN	Yeah, in life we were human beings, and at this stage, we're only shadows of our human being selves, so we're shadow beings.
ETHAN	We? You mean there are more of you? *(He looks around.)*
MARTIN	Don't worry. I'm the only one you'll see.

ETHAN   I'm asleep, aren't I? I dozed off and I'm
                dreaming.

MARTIN   I'm afraid not.

ETHAN   No, I am. I've been working hard late-
                ly. I'm just tired, that's all.

MARTIN   Take that spoon and stick it in the
                teapot, Ethan.

ETHAN   What?

MARTIN   Take the spoon there and stick it in the
                teapot.

ETHAN   Why?

MARTIN   Just do it.

                ETHAN sticks the spoon into the teapot.

ETHAN   All right, now what?

MARTIN   Just wait a second. *(Beat.)* Okay, take it
                out.

                ETHAN takes the spoon out.

                Now, touch the back of your hand with
                the spoon.

                ETHAN does it. The spoon burns.

ETHAN   Ow!!

MARTIN   Well, you're not dreaming. I guess I'm
                here.

ETHAN   But, why? What are you doing here?

MARTIN   Well, I'm not sure. I don't know a
                whole lot about my assignment yet. I

	just know it's going to happen here.
ETHAN	Assignment?
MARTIN	Yeah. I'm here to set somebody on the right path or something. Apparently, when you've wronged somebody in life, you have to do something good for someone after you die. Which is pretty unfair if you ask me, telling you the rules after the game is over.
ETHAN	Who did you wrong?
MARTIN	Ethan, I was a car salesman.
ETHAN	I can't believe this.
MARTIN	*You* can't believe it? A heart attack at forty-three years old. I thought only the good died young. *(looking at the painting)* This is back home, isn't it?
ETHAN	Hmm?
MARTIN	The painting. That's back home. The mountains, the Bedwell's house.... *(Beat.)* And the pond.
ETHAN	Yeah.
MARTIN	Hmm. *(He moves across the room to the kitchen counter.)* Ooh, bananas. Dad turned me into a banana addict. Remember that? "Eat your bananas, Martin. Your muscles need the potassium." He didn't tell me that too much potassium could also lead to heart trouble. Man, I ate about ten of those things every day until the day I died. I couldn't get enough.
ETHAN	Go ahead. Have one.

MARTIN	No.
ETHAN	Well, how about a sandwich? Can I fix you a sandwich?
MARTIN	Ethan, we don't eat.
ETHAN	You don't?
MARTIN	Don't eat, don't drink. Nothin'. Don't need to. Even if I wanted to I couldn't pick it up.
ETHAN	Why not?
MARTIN	I'm in the spirit world. I'm not a physical presence. I can't touch anything here.
ETHAN	Does that mean you can't... move something?
MARTIN	What do you mean?
ETHAN	You know? Levitate something.
MARTIN	Why do people think that as soon you die, you turn into David Copperfield?
ETHAN	So, what's it like in the spirit world?
MARTIN	Drafty.
ETHAN	Drafty?
MARTIN	Yeah, it's chilly. But, then I suppose somebody else is monopolizing all the heat.
ETHAN	I still can't believe this is happening.
MARTIN	So, how's the egg farming business?

ETHAN	Hmm? Oh, good. Good.
MARTIN	No, it's not.
ETHAN	Yes, it is.
MARTIN	Ethan, I know.
ETHAN	You do?
MARTIN:	Of course I do. So, what's the problem?
ETHAN	Well, I've got two thousand layers out there laying one egg a day. That's not enough to cover my costs any more.
MARTIN	So, get more hens.
ETHAN	Well, if I do that I've got to build another barn, buy more equipment. I haven't got the money for that.
MARTIN	One egg a day, huh? Bunch of under-achievers if you ask me. Well, not unlike yourself.
ETHAN	I've done all right.
MARTIN	The bank's gonna put a lien on your farm, Ethan. That doesn't sound all right to me.
ETHAN	The bank's not putting a lien on my farm. Who told you that?
	MARTIN just shrugs knowingly.
	They're putting a lien on my farm?
MARTIN	The notice went out in the mail on Friday. You'll get it tomorrow.
ETHAN	Well, what does it say?

MARTIN	(*thinking*) Well, let's see now. "Dear, Mr. Claymore. It has come to our attention that..."
ETHAN	Not the whole letter. Just the important part.
MARTIN	It says you've got until the end of the month to come up with five thousand dollars, or you lose the farm. You got five thousand dollars, Ethan?
ETHAN	No.
MARTIN	I know you don't.
ETHAN	I'll bet you're happy about that, aren't you, Martin?
MARTIN	Doesn't matter to me one way or the other.
ETHAN	When was the last time we talked?
MARTIN	Beats me.
ETHAN	It was fourteen years ago. Just before Jenny and I moved out here. Do you remember what you said to me then?
MARTIN	Can't say as I do.
ETHAN	You said you hoped I didn't mess up Jenny's life like I messed up yours. You made me feel guilty about that my whole life.
MARTIN	I wound up selling cars, Ethan. Don't talk to me about how *you* felt. How do you think I felt??
ETHAN	But, it wasn't my fault.

MARTIN	Hold it, hold it. *(He looks around as if he's heard something.)* I gotta go.
ETHAN	What? Go where?
MARTIN	I don't know. I just know I have to go.
ETHAN	Why?
MARTIN	They want to talk to me.
ETHAN	Who?
MARTIN	The ones who hand out the assignments.
ETHAN	And who are they?
MARTIN	Three women.
ETHAN	Women?
MARTIN	Yeah. And boy, are they giving me a hard time.
ETHAN	Well, are you coming back?
MARTIN	Oh, yeah. I'll be back. See you later. *(starts for the door)*
ETHAN	Well, when? When are you coming back?
MARTIN	I don't know. Soon. Why?
ETHAN	Well, I don't want you scaring me again like you did this time.
MARTIN	Fine. I'll give you some warning next time.
ETHAN	Wait, wait. How are you going to leave?

MARTIN	What do you mean?
ETHAN	Well, do you disappear? Do you walk through walls?
MARTIN	No, I don't walk through walls. That freaks me out. Makes me feel like Casper.
ETHAN	So, how do you leave?

The door opens on it's own, as if by magic.

MARTIN	All right, so we know a few tricks. So long, Nancy. I'll be in touch.

MARTIN exits. The door closes by itself. After a beat, YOUNG ETHAN enters through the front door in a panic.

YNG. ETHAN	Dad!! Dad!!
ETHAN	What is it, Ethan?
YNG. ETHAN	Dad, you've got to come to the pond. It's Martin.
ETHAN	Martin? What happened?
YNG. ETHAN	I didn't mean it, Dad. It wasn't my fault. Honest. Jim Bedwell pushed me.
ETHAN	All right, Ethan, calm down and tell me what happened.
YNG. ETHAN	I was playing defense—they tried to put me in goal, but I said no—so I was playing defense and Martin was coming in and I was just going to get out of his way because I didn't want to get hurt, but Jim Bedwell pushed me in front of him.

ETHAN	In front of Martin?
YNG. ETHAN	Yes. And we got all tangled up and Martin went down funny on his leg.
ETHAN	What do you mean funny?
YNG. ETHAN	Well, it got all twisted up like, underneath him. And now he can't walk.
ETHAN	All right, let's go. *(He moves to get his coat.)*
YNG. ETHAN	I didn't mean it, Dad. It's not my fault. Martin keeps saying it's my fault, but it was Jim Bedwell.
ETHAN	All right, Ethan, I know. But, I told you you shouldn't play with those boys. They're too big.
YNG. ETHAN	Jim Bedwell's a jerk.
ETHAN	Yes, he is. He always has been.
YNG. ETHAN	But, why? How does he get like that?
ETHAN	It's inherited, son. His father's a jerk. Maybe his grandfather too. I never met the man.

*ETHAN and YOUNG ETHAN exit.
Lights down.*

ACT ONE

Scene Four

TIME: The next afternoon. Tuesday, December 22nd.
PLACE: The same.

As the scene opens ETHAN and DOUGLAS enter. They are wearing their winter coats. ETHAN takes his coat off and hangs it up. DOUGLAS stares at him as he does this.

ETHAN   All right, Douglas, what is it?

DOUGLAS   What's what?

ETHAN   Well, you didn't say a word the whole way home and for you, that's not normal. Now, what's wrong?

DOUGLAS   What's wrong?

ETHAN   Yes, what's wrong?

DOUGLAS   All right, Ethan, I'll tell you what's wrong. I take you to the Fina station for a nice afternoon of friendly chit-chat with some friends of mine. A favourable way to pass the time I think. Always has been. Why should today be any different? And what do you do? You start talking about ghosts and reincarnation and life after death.

ETHAN   So?

DOUGLAS   Ethan, I told you, the rules are very clear. We talk about nothing at the Fina station. Nothing. We talk about Harvey Pelletier's rebuilt transmission.

Gordie Washburn's new shed. Sue Ann
Tuckey's planter's warts. We don't talk
about life after death at the Fina! You
scared the heck out of those fellas. Poor
Calvin darn near fell off his orange
crate. And Woody? When you started
in about the spirit world I thought he
was gonna choke on his Mountain Dew.

ETHAN   I didn't see anything wrong. I was just
          talking about whatever popped into my
          head.

DOUGLAS   Well, stop it. You keep those thoughts
          to yourself. Those fellas won't sleep for
          weeks now. They'll be afraid to close
          their eyes. And what the heck is a
          shadow being?

ETHAN   Well, it's what they call a...

DOUGLAS   Never mind! I don't want to know.

ETHAN   All right, next time I won't talk about
          anything of substance.

DOUGLAS   If there is a next time. Those boys
          might not want you coming back again.
          I mean, Robert got up to use the wash-
          room four times while you were there.
          He never goes that much. I think you
          upset his regulatory system.

ETHAN   All right, I'm sorry. Would you like a
          coffee?

DOUGLAS   Coffee?

ETHAN   Yes.

DOUGLAS   Coffee. Well, you know it's pretty cold
          out there, Ethan. It might be better if I

had something to warm me up for the trip home.

ETHAN   You live a hundred yards away.

DOUGLAS   Well, it is bitter cold.

ETHAN   You've got your truck.

DOUGLAS   Ethan, are you going to offer me a rum or not?

ETHAN   Of course I am. I just wanted to see you squirm.

> *ETHAN goes to the kitchen and takes out a bottle of rum. He pours a drink for DOUGLAS.*

DOUGLAS   Oh, I went over to Vicker's Rock to find you a Christmas tree this morning, but they didn't have what I'm looking for. And on the way back I checked into a lot in Hartsburg, but they were scrawny things, so, I think after supper I'll head down to Newton. Myrna Pollock's cousin Travis has got a tree lot down there next to his scrap yard.

ETHAN   You're going to buy a Christmas tree from a scrap dealer?

DOUGLAS   Well, now don't sell Travis short now. He's got quite a nativity scene set up down there. He's got an old rusted out DeSoto for a manger, and three little garden gnomes for the wise men. It's a real attraction. Speaking of attractions, the whole town is talking about your date with Miss Pike tomorrow night.

ETHAN   My what?

DOUGLAS	Your date. The party at the school.
ETHAN	Miss Pike and I don't have a date.
DOUGLAS	Well, you bought those new clothes yesterday.
ETHAN	I bought those new clothes because it was number one on your list.
DOUGLAS	Oh, that's why.
ETHAN	That's right. And I'm going to the party because you said I work too much. You said I should consort more. Fraternize, remember?
DOUGLAS	Oh, I see.
ETHAN	There's no date involved here. I'm going alone.
DOUGLAS	Of course you are.
ETHAN	I am.
DOUGLAS	In that truck of yours that doesn't work, I suppose.
ETHAN	No, I was going to ask you and Caroline for a ride.
DOUGLAS	Oh.
ETHAN	So, can I have one?
DOUGLAS	Of course, of course.
ETHAN	Thank you.
DOUGLAS	Unless you get a better offer before then.

ETHAN hands DOUGLAS his glass of rum.

Ah, there we go. Thank you. You're not having one?

ETHAN No.

DOUGLAS But, it's the festive season. You don't expect me to toast the season alone, do you?

ETHAN You don't want it then?

DOUGLAS That's not what I said.

ETHAN Well, if you don't want to drink alone I'll take it back. *(He reaches for the glass.)*

DOUGLAS Uh-uh-uh! As long as you've poured it I'll force myself. But, just this once. Season's greetings, Ethan. *(He raises his glass in a toast then drinks.)*

MARTIN *(off, in a ghostly howl)* Oooooooohhh. Oooooohhhh!!!

ETHAN What was that?

DOUGLAS What?

ETHAN That noise. Did you hear that?

DOUGLAS Oh, I'm sorry. I didn't pass gas, did I?

ETHAN No, no, no. Listen.

MARTIN *(Off.)* E-e-e-ethan Claymore!!!

ETHAN There. That.

DOUGLAS I didn't hear anything.

The door swings open and MARTIN enters.

MARTIN   How ya doin?

DOUGLAS   Ah. Must've been the wind you heard.

DOUGLAS moves to close the door.

ETHAN   *(to MARTIN)* What are you doing?

DOUGLAS   I'm closing the door. It's cold out there.

ETHAN   *(to MARTIN)* I said what are you doing?

DOUGLAS   *(loudly)* I'm closing the door! It's cold out there!

MARTIN   So, is that better?

DOUGLAS   *(after closing the door)* There that's better.

ETHAN   *(to MARTIN)* Better than what?

DOUGLAS   Well, better than leaving it open.

ETHAN   *(to DOUGLAS)* Uh... yes, thank you. That's much better.

DOUGLAS   You're welcome.

MARTIN   You said you wanted some warning.

ETHAN   *(to MARTIN)* I what?

DOUGLAS   You're welcome. Are you all right?

ETHAN   *(to DOUGLAS)* Uh... yes, yes. Fine.

DOUGLAS   Good. Come on, Ethan, let's sit for a bit. There's nothing like enjoying the

company of friends during the Yuletide.
(*He moves to a chair.*)

ETHAN   (*to DOUGLAS*) No!

DOUGLAS   What?

ETHAN   No, you can't sit.

DOUGLAS   Why not?

ETHAN   Uh... because I have things to do. And
          if you stay I'll never get to them.

DOUGLAS   What things?

ETHAN   I... have to clean the manure out of the
          chicken barn.

MARTIN   Oh, good one.

DOUGLAS   Now?

ETHAN   Yes. Right now.

DOUGLAS   But, I haven't finished my drink yet.

ETHAN   Take it with you.

DOUGLAS   What?

ETHAN   Take it with you.

DOUGLAS   But, it'll be finished in five minutes.

MARTIN   Let the man sit.

ETHAN   (*to MARTIN*) Oh, be quiet.

DOUGLAS   What?

ETHAN   Not you.

DOUGLAS	Not me what?
ETHAN	Nothing. Please Douglas, just go.
DOUGLAS	Are you throwing me out?
ETHAN	No, I'm not throwing you out. Of course not. *(He takes DOUGLAS by the arm and leads him up to the door.)*

The door swings open.

DOUGLAS	You know you oughta get the latch on that door fixed.
ETHAN	*(to MARTIN)* Will you cut that out?
DOUGLAS	Cut what out? I'm just giving you some friendly advice.
ETHAN	Yes, well, thank you, Douglas. I'll get it fixed right away.
DOUGLAS	After you clean up the manure you mean.
ETHAN	Right. *(in a friendly way)* Now, if you don't get out of here, Douglas Aloysius McLaren, I won't get anything done.
DOUGLAS	Well, all right. *(He steps outside the door with his drink in his hand.)* You go to it, Ethan. *(He stops outside and turns back to ETHAN.)* But, I swear. I've never seen a man so anxious to get to a pile of chicken...

The door swings closed before DOUGLAS can finish.

ETHAN	So, you're back.
MARTIN	That I am.

ETHAN	I was hoping you were just a dream. *(He goes to the counter and pours himself a rum.)*
MARTIN	No such luck.
ETHAN	So, did you find out about your assignment?
MARTIN	No, they're swamped right now. It's a busy season for redemption I guess. They just told me to sit tight and they'll get back to me. So, you got your notice from the bank.
ETHAN	Yeah, got it this morning, just like you said I would. *(He picks up a letter.)*
MARTIN	It's amazing how I know all this stuff, huh? I tell you, if I'd had this knowledge while I was still alive, I would've been a rich man. I'd know which horse was going to win at the track, what the lottery numbers would be.
ETHAN	Well, it's nice to see that you'd use that knowledge to help mankind.
MARTIN	Yeah, right. And what did mankind ever do to help me? Gave me a torn up knee and heart disease. Remind me to send it a thank you card.
ETHAN	You know, I would've thought that dead people wouldn't be bitter like that.
MARTIN	Wouldn't be bitter? We're dead. We're all bitter! I met a man here who lived til' he was a hundred and two. He thinks *he* got shortchanged.
ETHAN	Well, I would think that you'd be remorseful.

MARTIN	Ethan, I died and I lost a Riviera sale. It's been a bad week. Get the door.
ETHAN	What?

There is a knock on the door

MARTIN	Man, this is fun.
ETHAN	*(Moving to the door.)* And don't you distract me.
MARTIN	I won't say a word.
ETHAN	Don't even breathe.
MARTIN	I haven't for over a week now.

ETHAN opens the door. TERESA PIKE is there.

TERESA	Hello.
ETHAN	Oh, Teresa. Hi.
TERESA	Hi.
MARTIN	Hi.
TERESA	How are you today?
ETHAN	Fine.
MARTIN	I'm dead on my feet.
TERESA	Cold weather we're having.
ETHAN	Yes, it is.
MARTIN	Ethan, can't you take a hint? Invite her in.
ETHAN	Uh... would you like to come in?

TERESA	All right. But, just for a moment.
	TERESA enters. ETHAN closes the door.
	I just stopped by to ask you something.
ETHAN	Oh? And what's that?
TERESA	Well, I heard that your truck was broken down, and I was wondering if you'd be needing a ride tomorrow night.
MARTIN	Oh, she likes you.
ETHAN	Uh... well, actually Douglas McLaren and his wife have already offered me a ride.
TERESA	Oh.
MARTIN	What??!
TERESA	Well, all right then.
MARTIN	Are you out of your mind?
TERESA	So, you won't be needing one then?
MARTIN	Yes, he will.
ETHAN	No, I won't.
MARTIN	Yes, you will.
ETHAN	No, I won't!
TERESA	Fine.
MARTIN	Ethan, can I see you over by the stove please? *(He moves into the kitchen.)*
TERESA	Well, that's all I stopped by for then.

MARTIN	Ethan??
TERESA	Just wanted to make sure you weren't stranded here.
MARTIN	Ethan? Now!
ETHAN	*(to TERESA)* Uh... could you hold on for just a second, please? I have to check on something in the oven.
TERESA	Oh, certainly.

ETHAN moves to the kitchen. He opens the oven and looks in.

MARTIN	Ethan, who would you rather ride with? This woman here who, for some reason, seems to like you? Or Uncle Jed and Granny next door? I mean, do you think she goes around offering rides to everybody who has no transportation? Man, if I could kick your butt right now I would. *(looking skyward)* Come on, let me kick him once! Just once!

ETHAN closes the oven and moves back to TERESA.

Say, yes, Ethan. Or I'll haunt you for the rest of your life.

TERESA	Everything okay?
ETHAN	Yes, perfect.
TERESA	Cooking supper, are you?
ETHAN	Yes.
TERESA	Funny, I don't smell anything. It doesn't even look like the oven's on.

ETHAN	No, well, it's steak tartar.
MARTIN	Oh, nice save.
ETHAN	You know, Teresa, maybe I will accept your kind offer of a ride.
TERESA	Oh. All right.
MARTIN	There you go.
TERESA	I'll pick you up on my way to get Mr. and Mrs. Olmstead.
ETHAN	Mr. and Mrs. Olmstead?
TERESA	Yes, they both have failing eyesight and they can't drive. And then we have to pick up Harvey Pelletier. He's having his transmission rebuilt. You see, the school thought we should offer rides to anyone who doesn't have transportation.
ETHAN	Oh, I see.
TERESA	So, I'll be by tomorrow about seven-thirty?

TERESA moves to the door. ETHAN opens it for her.

ETHAN	Seven-thirty. Good.
TERESA	Good. Well, see you then.
ETHAN	Goodbye.
MARTIN	*(waving)* Tartar.

ETHAN closes the door.

ETHAN	You knew, didn't you?

MARTIN	Of course I knew. I know everything.
ETHAN	You're not a very nice person in death either, are you?
MARTIN	Hey, is that any way to talk to your brother who loves you?
ETHAN	I have to go. *(He gets his coat.)*
MARTIN	Go? Go where?
ETHAN	The manure is piling up. *(He opens the door.)* It's piling up in the chicken barn too. *(He exits.)*
MARTIN	*(to himself)* The kid never could take a joke.

YOUNG MARTIN enters from the bedroom. He is limping badly. He sits in the chair. YOUNG ETHAN enters, wearing a winter coat and carrying a small artist's canvas and a book bag.

YNG. ETHAN	How ya feeling?
YNG. MARTIN	How do you think I'm feeling? I'll never play hockey again, that's how I'm feeling.
YNG. ETHAN	Well, at least you don't have to stay in the hospital over Christmas. You should be happy about that.
YNG. MARTIN	Leave me alone.
YNG. ETHAN	Martin, it wasn't my fault.
YNG. MARTIN	Get lost.
YNG. ETHAN	*(He puts his canvas into the bag.)* You want me to bring you something back?

YNG. MARTIN Where are you going?

YNG. ETHAN I have to take my painting of Mom over to Mr. Hoffman's to get it framed. If I don't get it over there today it won't be ready for Christmas. So, do you want anything?

YNG. MARTIN No.

YNG. ETHAN I can go to the library and get you a book if you want.

YNG. MARTIN I said no.

YNG. ETHAN Okay. *(checking his coat pockets)* Where are my gloves?

YNG. MARTIN How should I know where your stupid gloves are?

YNG. ETHAN They must be in my room. *(He exits to his room.)*

> *YOUNG MARTIN gets up from the chair. He takes the canvas out of YOUNG ETHAN's bag, he bends it in half and throws it into the woodstove, then sits again. YOUNG ETHAN enters, putting his gloves on. He picks up his bag.*

YNG. ETHAN Well, see ya later.

> *YOUNG MARTIN doesn't answer. YOUNG ETHAN starts for the door. When he gets to the door, he stops.*

Martin, I'm really sorry you hurt yourself so bad. I mean it. I wish it was me who got hurt cause' I don't care about hockey like you do. I don't care if can play or not and I know you do. I'm really sorry, okay?

YOUNG MARTIN doesn't answer.

Okay, Martin?

ETHAN exits. YOUNG MARTIN stares straight ahead. MARTIN stands behind him and stares out. Lights down.

End Act One.

ACT TWO

Scene One

TIME: Wednesday, December 23rd.
PLACE: The same.

As the scene opens there is no one on stage. The door to the home swings open and MARTIN enters. The door swings closed behind him.

MARTIN   *(to himself)* What a lousy party that was. No alcohol, no dancing. How do the Amish do it?

There is a crash of thunder and a flash of lightning. MARTIN looks up.

It was a joke! I'm joking! Boy, for a person who gave us the ostrich, you don't have much of a sense of humour. By the way, I've been meaning to ask you, what happened to this light you're supposed to see when you're dying? You know, I heard you're supposed to walk towards the light. Well, I didn't see any light. I was fumbling around in the dark there for a good twenty minutes.

MARTIN wanders over and looks at the painting.

I wish I could go back there. No second chances I guess, huh? *(Beat, as he waits for an answer.)* No, I didn't think so.

YOUNG MARTIN enters from the bedroom. He limps to a chair and sits. The door opens and YOUNG ETHAN rushes in.

YNG. ETHAN	Dad?? Dad!!
	ETHAN enters from the bedroom.
ETHAN	What's wrong?
YNG. ETHAN	Dad, I lost my painting.
ETHAN	What?
YNG. ETHAN	My painting of Mom. It's gone.
ETHAN	Gone? How could you lose it?
YNG. ETHAN	I don't know. I put it in my bag, and I thought I zipped it shut, but maybe I didn't. I don't know. And when I was running to Mr. Hoffman's, it must've fallen out I guess.
ETHAN	Oh, Ethan.
YNG. ETHAN	Dad, what am I gonna do? That was my Christmas present for Mom.
ETHAN	All right, all right. *(He gets his coat and puts it on.)* We'll find it. Which way did you go? Past the pond, or through the woods?
YNG. ETHAN	The woods.
ETHAN	All right, we'll just retrace your steps then.
YNG. ETHAN	But, I already looked.
ETHAN	Well, we'll look again.
MARTIN	*(to YOUNG MARTIN)* Tell them.
ETHAN	Now, you went straight there, did you? You didn't go anywhere else first?

YNG. ETHAN   No, I went straight there.

ETHAN   All right then. We'll find it.

MARTIN   *(to YOUNG MARTIN)* Tell them.

ETHAN   Martin, we'll be right back. Come on, Ethan.

YOUNG ETHAN and ETHAN exit. MARTIN moves to YOUNG MARTIN.

MARTIN   Get up. Call them back.

YOUNG MARTIN doesn't hear.

Get up, you coward!

YOUNG MARTIN gets out of the chair and moves to the front door. He opens it.

Call them. Go on. They can still hear you.

YOUNG MARTIN says nothing.

Call them!

MARTIN steps outside and yells.

Dad!! Ethan!! Come back! I took the painting!! It was me!! Dad!!?

YOUNG MARTIN turns away from the door. He moves toward the bedroom. MARTIN turns and looks at him from outside.

I hate you.

A flash of lightning and a crash of thunder. The door swings closed. The door opens and ETHAN enters. He is wearing the

*clothes he purchased at Erdie's. Nice
slacks and a shirt under his winter coat.
He looks outside as he enters.*

ETHAN *(to himself)* Awfully cold weather for
thunder and lightning. *(He looks around
the room.)* Martin... Martin, are you
here? Are you anywhere? *(He hangs up
his coat.)*

MARTIN enters from the bedroom.

MARTIN What is it?

ETHAN is startled.

ETHAN Geez! Don't do that. It's bad enough
when real people sneak up on you, let
alone a... someone like you.

MARTIN You were going to say ghost, weren't
you?

ETHAN Well, to my mind, that's what you are.
That's what we've been told all our
lives. Dead people who come back are
ghosts.

MARTIN And I suppose you're too old to change,
huh?

ETHAN Don't talk to me about changing,
Martin. Even dying couldn't change
you.

MARTIN So, where's your date?

ETHAN What?

MARTIN Your date. The woman.

ETHAN She wasn't my date.

MARTIN	Whatever. Where is she?
ETHAN	She's on her way home.
MARTIN	What?
ETHAN	She's on her way home. She dropped me off and went home.
MARTIN	You didn't invite her in?
ETHAN	No.
MARTIN	Well, what's the matter with you? She wanted you to invite her in.
ETHAN	She did?
MARTIN	Of course she did. She likes you.
ETHAN	But she only gave me a ride tonight because it was school policy.
MARTIN	The school policy was an *excuse* to give you a ride, you bonehead. Man, you make me mad sometimes. You just don't catch on, do you?
ETHAN	Catch on to what?
MARTIN	You're naive, Ethan. You always have been. You don't know it when somebody likes you and you don't know it when somebody's trying to hurt you. You make me sick.
ETHAN	What are you getting so angry about?
MARTIN	Forget it. What's the point?
ETHAN	*(Beat.)* You mean she *does* like me.
MARTIN	Never mind. Get the door.

DOUGLAS enters.

DOUGLAS	Ethan?
MARTIN	Oh, right. He never knocks.
ETHAN	Hello, Douglas.
DOUGLAS	Where's your date?
ETHAN	She wasn't my date. And she's on her way home.
DOUGLAS	What, you didn't invite her in?
MARTIN	You see?
ETHAN	No, Douglas, I didn't invite her in.
DOUGLAS	Why not? She likes you.
ETHAN	Well, I didn't know she liked me.
DOUGLAS	She gave you a ride tonight, didn't she?
ETHAN	I thought the ride was school policy. I didn't know the school policy was an excuse to give me a ride.
DOUGLAS	I thought everybody knew it was an excuse. Everybody at the party knew.
ETHAN	Well, I missed the signal I guess.
DOUGLAS	Gee, you'd have to be a bonehead to miss that signal.
MARTIN	I'm starting to like this guy.
DOUGLAS	Anyway, I've got something for you, Ethan. *(He takes a cheque out of his pocket.)*

ETHAN   What's that?

DOUGLAS   Caroline and I want you to take this.
              You can pay us back whenever you
              want. No rush.

ETHAN   Five thousand dollars?

DOUGLAS   Now, it's not charity. That's a loan. I
              don't want you to think we're taking
              pity on you.

ETHAN   How did you know I needed five thou-
              sand dollars?

DOUGLAS   Everybody knows.

ETHAN   But, this is bank business. Isn't that
              supposed to be confidential?

DOUGLAS   How long have you lived here, Ethan?
              When one of us is in trouble, we're all in
              trouble, and that makes it everybody's
              business, you oughta know that.

ETHAN   Well, I appreciate this, Douglas, but...

DOUGLAS   Uh-uh-uh. Never mind. I'm not doing
              it for you anyway. I'm doing it for me.
              I mean, if you're forced out of here
              there's no telling what kind of neigh-
              bours I'll get next. (*He moves to the
              kitchen area.*) They might be a bunch of
              snobs, or moochers, or God forbid, tee-
              totalers. (*He takes the bottle of rum out of
              the cupboard and pours himself a drink.*)
              Oh, by the way, I'm still working on
              that Christmas tree, Ethan. I went
              down to Travis Pollock's tree lot yester-
              day but his selection was limited. Got
              to see that nativity scene though so it
              wasn't a total loss. And then this after-
              noon I tried a couple of lots over in

Kelly's Junction but they didn't have the perfect tree either. Tomorrow though. I'll get you one tomorrow for sure. Cheers. *(He drinks.)*

ETHAN   Douglas...

There is a knock on the door.

MARTIN   Oh, now who could that be?

ETHAN opens the door. TERESA is there.

TERESA   Hello, Ethan, I'm sorry to bother you. I haven't caught you at a bad time I hope.

ETHAN   No.

TERESA   Good. I can't believe this.

ETHAN   What's wrong?

MARTIN & DOUGLAS   Invite her in!!

ETHAN   Uh... come in, please.

TERESA   Oh, thank you.

MARTIN   *(to DOUGLAS)* Kid's as thick as a brick.

TERESA enters. ETHAN closes the door.

ETHAN   So, what's the problem?

TERESA   Well... oh, hello, Douglas.

DOUGLAS   Miss Pike.

TERESA   Well, the strangest thing just happened. I pulled out onto the highway there and my car died.

ETHAN   What?

TERESA   Just quit for no reason. Like someone
               turned off the ignition or something.

DOUGLAS   Sounds like the alternator to me.

MARTIN   That'd be my guess too.

TERESA   So, I was wondering if I could use your
               phone to call a tow truck?

DOUGLAS   Oh, no need for that. I'll give you a ride
               home, Miss Pike. We can look after that
               car of yours tomorrow.

MARTIN   Yeah, it'll probably start tomorrow.

TERESA   Oh, well, that's very kind of you,
               Douglas.

ETHAN   That might not be a good idea, Douglas.
               I mean, you have been drinking.

DOUGLAS   Oh, right. Well, I'll tell you what then.
               I'll call Caroline and she can drive you
               home, Miss Pike.

TERESA   Thank you. That's very kind.

               DOUGLAS moves to the phone.

MARTIN   Here's a better idea, Doug.

DOUGLAS   Actually, I've got a better idea. I'll walk
               over and get Caroline.

ETHAN   Why? Why not just phone her ?

DOUGLAS   Well... because.

ETHAN   Because why?

DOUGLAS	Because I don't want to.
ETHAN	Why not?
DOUGLAS	Because if I walk over, it'll take longer and it'll give you two some time alone. Now, isn't that a good idea?
MARTIN	It's a great idea.
DOUGLAS	See you in a bit.
	DOUGLAS exits.
ETHAN	*(to TERESA)* I'm sorry about that.
TERESA	It seems the good people of Gladden's Head are determined to get us together somehow.
ETHAN	Oh, you've noticed, have you??
TERESA	Oh, yes. I guess no one thinks that a person can be alone in this world. Everybody's got to be attached, you know?
ETHAN	Yeah.
TERESA	Especially around Christmastime. Nobody likes to think that someone's going to spend Christmas alone.
MARTIN	Offer her a seat.
ETHAN	*(to MARTIN)* I was going to.
TERESA	Going to what?
ETHAN	Spend Christmas alone.
TERESA	Yes, me too.

ETHAN   Would you like to sit?

TERESA   Oh, thank you.

               TERESA sits. There is a pause.

ETHAN   Well.

MARTIN   *(to ETHAN)* Hello?? What about a
               drink? Something to take the chill off?

ETHAN   Would you like a drink? Rum and
               eggnog?

TERESA   Oh, all right. That'd be nice. But, only
               if you're having one.

ETHAN   Sure, I'll have one. *(He moves to the
               cupboard to get the drinks.)* Too bad
               about your car.

TERESA   Yes. *(Beat.)* It really did die on me. I
               mean, I didn't make that up just to...
               you know... so, I could come back here
               and...

ETHAN   No, I believe you. I'm sure it did die.
               (looking at MARTIN) In fact, I know it
               did. *(Beat.)* So, you're spending
               Christmas alone. You've got no family
               to spend it with?

TERESA   No, my parents spend every Christmas
               in Florida. They invited me to come
               down, but Christmas in Florida
               wouldn't seem like Christmas to me.

ETHAN   No brothers or sisters?

TERESA   No, I'm an only child I'm afraid.

ETHAN   Well, now, there's a lot to be said for
               being an only child.

MARTIN   Watch it.

TERESA   Well, I always wished I had a sister.

MARTIN   I did have a sister. Right, Nancy?

TERESA   It would've been nice to have had
          someone to share my childhood with.
          An older sister that I could learn from.
          Look up to. I think we would've been
          very close.

          ETHAN gives TERESA her drink.

          Thank you. So, you and your brother,
          you weren't close?

ETHAN   Not really.

TERESA   Why not?

ETHAN   *(Beat.)* I don't know. Things happened.
          (changing the subject) So, you've never
          been married?

TERESA   No.

ETHAN   Well, that's surprising. An attractive,
          intelligent woman like you. No man's
          ever proposed to you?

          TERESA doesn't answer.

MARTIN   Oh-oh. Sore spot.

ETHAN   *(to TERESA)* I'm sorry. Is that a sore
          spot?

MARTIN   Isn't that what I just said?

ETHAN   *(to MARTIN)* Do you mind?

TERESA   No, I don't mind. I'm over it now. I

was engaged. We were supposed to be married in June, but... well, I got cold feet. I realized that he wasn't the one I wanted to spend the rest of my life with. I guess I'm looking for the perfect man. Like Douglas and your Christmas tree I guess.

ETHAN   You know about that, huh?

TERESA   The whole town knows.

ETHAN   So, you broke off the engagement?

TERESA   Actually, I broke off the wedding.

ETHAN   You what?

TERESA   Yeah. Right there at the church.

ETHAN   You got as far as the church?

TERESA   Oh, further. In fact, all the way to the part where the minister says "If anyone here knows of any reason why these two should not be joined together, let them speak now or forever hold their peace."

ETHAN   And then what?

TERESA   Well, I put up my hand.

ETHAN   You didn't.

TERESA   I did. I mean, I had to. I looked around and saw that nobody else was going to. And it would've been unfair to me and to my fiancé to go through with it, so, I thanked everyone for coming, walked out of the church, flagged down a cab and here I am.

ETHAN	Wow.
TERESA	Yeah, wow. But, like I say, I'm pretty much over it now. *(She takes a big drink of her rum and eggnog.)* I understand it's taken you quite a while to get over your wife's death. That's what I'm told anyway.
ETHAN	Uh... well...
TERESA	Oh, I'm sorry. I shouldn't have brought that up.
ETHAN	No, that's okay. Jenny and I were... well, we were very much in love. I don't think you ever get over feelings like that.
TERESA	No, I guess not. But, you don't stop living either. I mean, I don't think you do. I don't know. I've never been in that position.
MARTIN	Come on, Ethan, make your move. The old man's gonna be back soon.
ETHAN	*(Beat.)* So... uh... do you enjoy teaching at the school here?
TERESA	Oh, yes. Very much. The people are very friendly here.
ETHAN	Yes, they are, aren't they?
TERESA	Yes.
ETHAN	Very friendly.
TERESA	*(Beat.)* And you? You enjoy living here?
ETHAN	Yeah. Yeah.

MARTIN	Oh, man, this is killing me all over again.
TERESA	*(She stands.)* All right, look, we haven't got much time. Douglas is going to be back here soon, and I was just wondering if you'd like to have Christmas dinner at my house?

Beat, as ETHAN looks at MARTIN.

ETHAN	Uh...
MARTIN	Hey, I didn't make her do it. This is her idea.
TERESA	Well?
ETHAN	Uh... Christmas dinner?
TERESA	Yes, at my house.
ETHAN	With you?
TERESA	Well, I was planning on being there.
ETHAN	Well, uh... I don't know.
MARTIN	*(looking up)* Come on, just one kick in the butt. Please!
TERESA	All right, if you don't want to, that's okay. I didn't mean to put you on the spot. I'm sorry.
ETHAN	No, I'd like to.
TERESA	You would?
ETHAN	Yes. I'd like that very much.
MARTIN	Well, hallelujah!!!

TERESA	Well, good. All right then.
ETHAN	Good.

There is an awkward pause.

TERESA	Oh, what the heck!

She moves forward and gives ETHAN a quick kiss.

ETHAN	(*Beat.*) More eggnog?
MARTIN	Oh, yeah. That's her way of asking for more eggnog.

The door opens and DOUGLAS enters.

DOUGLAS	All right, Miss Pike. We're all set.
TERESA	Oh, all right. Good.
DOUGLAS	You two have a nice chat?
TERESA	Yes.
ETHAN	Yes.
DOUGLAS	Uh-huh. Would you like more time? There's no rush.
ETHAN	Just take the lady home, would you, Douglas?
DOUGLAS	Sure. Sure.

TERESA moves to the door.

TERESA	Well, goodnight. Again.
ETHAN	Yes, goodnight.
TERESA	See you soon. (*She exits.*)

DOUGLAS   *(to TERESA as he follows her out)* How soon? Do you know how soon?

   DOUGLAS exits.

MARTIN   Well, looks like your troubles are over, huh?

ETHAN   Why?

MARTIN   Well, you've got a date for Christmas dinner. You've got your five thousand dollars. You're set.

ETHAN   *(picking up the cheque)* I can't take this.

MARTIN   Why not?

ETHAN   Douglas and Caroline aren't doing much better than I am. This is probably all the money they've got. *(He tears up the cheque.)*

MARTIN   What are you doing?

ETHAN   I'll get out of this mess on my own.

MARTIN   No, you won't.

ETHAN   Then I'll go bankrupt. Whatever. I'm not going to take a friend's money. Dad used to say family and friends are the two most important things in life, remember? Well, at this point, I don't have any family to count on and I'll be damned if I'm going to jeopardize my friendships.

MARTIN   No family, huh? What about me?

ETHAN   That's funny, Martin. That's very funny.

   ETHAN exits to his room.

ETHAN	*(off)* Ethan?
	YOUNG ETHAN enters from ETHAN's room. ETHAN follows him.
	Ethan, where are you going?
YNG. ETHAN	I just want to go and look one more time.
ETHAN	Ethan, you've looked a hundred times already. It's gone.
YNG. ETHAN	Well, maybe I'll find it this time. Maybe it's...
ETHAN	Ethan, no. It's Christmas Eve. You lost that painting days ago.
YNG. ETHAN	I know, but maybe if I...
ETHAN	No buts. It's gone. Now, you're not going out there again. It's dark out there.
YNG. ETHAN	I'll take a flashlight.
ETHAN	I said no. Now, that's that.
YNG. ETHAN	But, I haven't got a present for Mom. And I told her I was making her something real special.
ETHAN	Well, I offered to give you the money to buy her something else.
YNG. ETHAN	No, I wanted to give her my painting.
ETHAN	Ethan, she'll understand. I promise you. The fact that you went to all that trouble to paint her portrait in the first place—that you wanted to do that for her—that'll be enough, believe me.

	Now, if you didn't get me a present, that'd be a different story. You did get me one, didn't you?
YNG. ETHAN	It's not funny, Dad. I've ruined every-body's Christmas.
ETHAN	Oh, don't be silly.
YNG. ETHAN	I have. I haven't got a present for Mom. I made Martin get hurt. I messed up everything.
ETHAN	No, you didn't. Martin will get over it. He just needs time.
YNG. ETHAN	No, he won't. He won't get over it. He hates me.
ETHAN	No. No, Martin loves you, and don't you ever forget that. You hear? I will not have that kind of talk in this house. Family and friends, Ethan. They're the most important things in life. We'll always be there for you. You under-stand that? Always.

YOUNG ETHAN doesn't answer.

Come here, son.

YOUNG ETHAN rushes to ETHAN and hugs him. Lights down.

ACT TWO

Scene Two

TIME: The next morning. Thursday, December 24th.
PLACE: The same.

As the scene opens, MARTIN is onstage.
He is looking out the window.

MARTIN   *(to himself)* Stupid snow. *(looking up)*
Don't get me wrong. It's beautiful if
you like that kind of thing, but we used
to hate snow when we were dealing
cars. Nobody buys in the snow. All the
sales guys would stand around the
showroom with their thumbs up their....
With their thumbs up. *(He gives the
thumbs up sign.)* "Tomorrow. We'll do
better tomorrow."

     *ETHAN enters from the bedroom. He's
wearing his overalls now.*

     Morning, Ethan.

ETHAN   Still here, huh?

MARTIN   Only in spirit.

ETHAN   No word on your assignment yet? *(He
heads to the kitchen area.)*

MARTIN   No. Listen, there's no time for breakfast
this morning, Ethan. You'd better go
out and check your chicken barn.

ETHAN   What for?

MARTIN   Well, there was an awful ruckus out
there last night. That's what you coun-

	try folk call it, isn't it? A ruckus?
ETHAN	What do you mean? What happened?
MARTIN	Well, you'd better go and have a look. It sounded plum serious though.
ETHAN	Well, what is it?
MARTIN	Just go and look, would you? Go. Go.

ETHAN moves to put his coat and boots on.

ETHAN	Well, I don't know why you can't just tell me. I mean, you know everything. Why can't you tell me?
MARTIN	No, this is something you're gonna have to see for yourself. Now, git.

ETHAN exits out the front door.

(*looking up*) So, this is it, huh? After this I have to go? (*Beat.*) Because if you don't need me right away, I thought maybe I could stay around for Christmas morning. Would that be all right? I mean, we haven't spent Christmas morning together in a lot of years. Not that it matters that much. I just thought as long as I'm here anyway. (*Beat.*) All right, it does matter, okay? Is that what you want to hear? It's only another twenty-four hours. Come on. (*Beat.*) Hello? Anybody? (*Beat.*) I'll take that as a no.

ETHAN enters the house.

ETHAN	What happened out there?! How could that happen?!

MARTIN	What's the matter?
ETHAN	Eggs. Eggs everywhere. There must be ten... twenty thousand of them out there.
MARTIN	Sixty.
ETHAN	Sixty?? Sixty thousand eggs?!
MARTIN	That's right.
ETHAN	But, that's impossible. I've got two thousand layers. They lay one egg a day!
MARTIN	Well, they were working overtime last night.
ETHAN	But, they couldn't have. They.... They'd have to lay thirty eggs each.
MARTIN	And that they did.
ETHAN	Thirty eggs. This is incredible. Was this your doing?
MARTIN	I put in a request, yeah.
ETHAN	Oh, my God. What am I gonna do?
MARTIN	Well, you've got sixty thousand eggs out there, and at the going rate for eggs, I'd say you'll have your five thousand dollars with some to spare.
ETHAN	But, my cooler's not big enough to hold sixty thousand eggs. I have to get them to the grading station today. Now.
MARTIN	Well, go.

ETHAN rushes for the door, then rushes back.

ETHAN   My truck's not working.

MARTIN   Wait a minute. *(Beat.)* Now it is.

ETHAN   It is?

MARTIN   Better than ever.

ETHAN rushes for the door again and comes back again.

ETHAN   My truck's not big enough to carry all those eggs. I'm going to need help. Douglas! I'll call Douglas. *(He rushes to the phone.)* Thirty eggs apiece. Are those chickens gonna be all right?

MARTIN   Well, they'll sleep for a while.

ETHAN   *(to the phone)* Douglas? Douglas, I need your help. I need you to get your truck over here right now... I'll explain when you get here. You won't believe it. And call anybody else who has a truck and ask them to come too...All right. Hurry. *(He hangs up.)* I'd better get out there and get loading. *(He exits.)*

ETHAN enters again and stands in the doorway.

MARTIN   What's wrong?

ETHAN   ...Thanks.

MARTIN   Just go, would ya?

ETHAN exits. Lights down.

ACT TWO

Scene Three

TIME: That evening. Christmas Eve.
PLACE: The same.

As the scene opens, ETHAN and TERESA
enter.

TERESA   Well, that was quite a day.

ETHAN   You can say that again.

TERESA   I've never seen that many eggs.

ETHAN   Listen, thanks again for helping out. I
                    really appreciate it.

TERESA   Oh, it was my pleasure. It gave me
                    something to do today. Christmas Eve,
                    you know. Another one of those days
                    when you don't like to sit around by
                    yourself.

ETHAN   Can I get you anything? Coffee? Tea?
                    Hot chocolate?

TERESA   Ooh, a hot chocolate would go nice
                    now.

ETHAN   All right.

ETHAN moves to the kitchen. TERESA
moves to the easel and looks at the
painting. ETHAN looks around the room
expecting MARTIN to show up.

TERESA   You haven't done any more work on
                    your painting.

ETHAN   Uh... no, well, it's been a busy week. *(whispering)* Martin? ...Martin, are you here? Where are you?

TERESA   Pardon me?

ETHAN   Uh... nothing. I was just wondering out loud where Douglas was. He left us very mysteriously a while ago. I just wonder where he went. *(He plugs in the kettle for hot chocolate.)*

TERESA   He went to get your Christmas tree.

ETHAN   What? You mean he's still on about that?

TERESA   Yes. He was so wrapped up in this egg mission that he forgot about it. He told me he had one more place to check and that's where he went.

ETHAN   That man. He's stubborn as a mule.

TERESA   He's a good friend.

ETHAN   Yes, he is.

TERESA   And he cares about you very much. You're lucky.

ETHAN   I know. What about you? Do you have any close friends in town?

TERESA   Not really close. Not yet. I take my time when it comes to choosing friends.

ETHAN   Well, if things work out, I could be one.

TERESA   What, a friend? Oh, no, I've got other plans for you. *(Beat.)* That.... That was out loud, wasn't it?

ETHAN   Yes.

TERESA   Sorry.

ETHAN   No, that's okay. I like a woman who
               says what's on her mind. Even when
               she doesn't know she's saying it.

TERESA   Oh.

ETHAN   I like it very much. My wife was like
               that. You always knew where you
               stood with Jenny.

TERESA   I see. Well, as long as you like that sort
               of thing, then maybe this won't be so
               hard for me to say.

ETHAN   What won't?

TERESA   Ethan, I... uh... I'm not an outgoing per-
               son really. Not very gregarious.

ETHAN   You're shy.

TERESA   That's exactly what I am. I'm shy. So,
               when it comes to starting a relation-
               ship—meeting a man that is—well, I'm
               not very good at it. Oh, sure, I was
               engaged, but it took us forever to get to
               that point, and even then he was the
               wrong guy. I mean, I don't know how
               many good men I might have missed
               out on because I was afraid to say, "Hey,
               I think you're cute" or "Hey, how about
               buying me a drink, tall boy?" I just can't
               do that. I can't. So, when I met you, I
               thought, well, this time it's going to be
               different. This time, I'm going to take
               the initiative. So, I invited you to the
               parents Christmas party. I invited you
               to my place for Christmas dinner. I
               even kissed you. On the mouth I kissed

you! But, gee whiz, Ethan, I can't do all
the work. You're going to have pitch in
here once in a while too. Now, I know
you've still got your wife on your mind.
Maybe that's what's holding you back, I
don't know. And if it is... I mean, if it's
still too soon for you, then just say so
and I'll back off. I'll back right off. But,
if it isn't – I mean, if you're interested in
getting something going here then holy
Hanna, do something will you?

She sits, worn out.

ETHAN   *(Beat.)* I am interested.

TERESA   You are?

ETHAN   Yes.

TERESA   Well, what are you going to do about it?

*ETHAN moves to TERESA. They move
in for a kiss but before they can, the door
opens and DOUGLAS enters. He is not
happy.*

DOUGLAS   Ethan, I've got your tree. And I don't
want to hear a peep out of either one of
you. Not a word, you understand?

ETHAN   Well, where is it?

DOUGLAS   It's right outside.

ETHAN   Well, aren't you going to bring it in?

DOUGLAS   Well, of course I am, you horse's hiney.
I just wanted to warn you first about
keeping your smartaleck comments to
yourself. Both of you. All right?

ETHAN   Fine.

TERESA	Fine.
DOUGLAS	Fine.

DOUGLAS exits and then returns with a scrawny tree on a stand.

	There. There's your Christmas tree. There's your festive pile of kindling!
ETHAN	What happened?
DOUGLAS	I left it too long that's what happened. It was the last tree I could find. Oh, yeah, there's more. *(He starts for the door.)*
ETHAN	Well, I hope there's more.
DOUGLAS	No, not more tree! That's it. That's the tree. All of it. I meant there's something else.
ETHAN	Oh.

DOUGLAS exits and returns with a cardboard box.

DOUGLAS	Here. Caroline sent some ornaments over. *(He drops the box on the floor.)* Feliz Navidad. *(He turns to exit.)*
ETHAN	Douglas, wait.
DOUGLAS	What?
ETHAN	I think it's a great tree.
DOUGLAS	Well, then you're a nut.
TERESA	No, Douglas, I think it's a nice tree too. Once we dress it up, it'll look beautiful.

ETHAN	Now, stay. Have some hot chocolate with us. Help us decorate it.
DOUGLAS	Well, just for a while. Caroline's expecting me.
ETHAN	Just for a while then.
TERESA	Now, let's see what we've got in here. *(TERESA opens up the box of ornaments.)*
	DOUGLAS moves to the kitchen area with ETHAN while TERESA starts decorating the tree.
ETHAN	Well, we put in quite a day's work today, didn't we?
DOUGLAS	We did that.
ETHAN	And all the people who showed up to help. I couldn't believe it.
DOUGLAS	It's like I said, Ethan, when one of us is trouble, we're all in trouble. Now, can I ask you something?
ETHAN	Yes, Douglas, you can have some rum in your hot chocolate.
DOUGLAS	No, it's not about that, and make it a double. No, what I want to know is, how in the heck did you get sixty thousand eggs out of two thousand chickens without a shoehorn??
ETHAN	You wouldn't believe me if I told you.
DOUGLAS	No, well, try me.
ETHAN	You really want to know?
DOUGLAS	Well, of course I do. Sixty thousand

eggs. The entire scientific community wants to know.

ETHAN   My brother Martin did it.

DOUGLAS   Come again.

ETHAN   My brother Martin. He put in a request and it was granted.

DOUGLAS   Your brother Martin?

ETHAN   That's right.

DOUGLAS   The dead brother?

ETHAN   Yes. He came back. He's been here since Monday.

DOUGLAS   He came back from where?

ETHAN   Well, he didn't actually come back. I mean, he didn't come back to life.

DOUGLAS   Oh, good.

ETHAN   No, he came here on his way to wherever you go after you die. Heaven I guess. I don't know. But, he stopped in here because he was in the area for an assignment, which he didn't get yet, but which they told him to sit tight for.

               Outside comes the sound of carolers singing, "Joy To The World."

               He has to put somebody on the right path, you see. Now, he's not a ghost, mind you. No, they don't like it when you call them that...

TERESA   Oh, listen. Listen. Carolers. Isn't that lovely?

DOUGLAS moves to the door. He opens it and shouts at the carolers.

DOUGLAS   Go away!!

The carolers stop. DOUGLAS closes the door, and moves back to ETHAN. TERESA looks out the window.

Now, I've warned you about this, haven't I, Ethan? About this life after death, spirit world stuff?

ETHAN   But, it's true.

DOUGLAS   Shhhh! You didn't mention any of this to Miss Pike, did you?

ETHAN   Well, no, but...

DOUGLAS   Good! You start talking like that around her and she'll be gone before you can say Ouija board. Now, let's hear no more about it, all right?

ETHAN   But, Douglas...

DOUGLAS   Uh-uh-uh!! No more. Please. Now, how's that hot chocolate coming?

ETHAN   Just about ready.

DOUGLAS   Good. Miss Pike, let me give you a hand there.

DOUGLAS moves to TERESA and begins decorating the tree. The door swings open and Martin enters. DOUGLAS moves to close the door.

You didn't get that latch fixed like I told you, Ethan.

ETHAN has his back to the door as he fixes the hot chocolate.

ETHAN   *(turning)* Hmm? *(He sees MARTIN.)* Martin.

DOUGLAS   What's that?

ETHAN   Uh... in the morning. I'll fix it in the morning.

DOUGLAS closes the door.

DOUGLAS   There we go. *(He returns to decorating the tree.)*

MARTIN   Well, it's about time you three got back. How'd the egg thing go?

ETHAN   Good.

MARTIN   So, you're all set now?

ETHAN   All set.

DOUGLAS   What was that?

ETHAN   I said all set. Are we all set for hot chocolate over there?

DOUGLAS   You bet we are. Bring it on.

MARTIN   Listen, Nancy, I just came to say good-bye. I have to go.

ETHAN   What?

MARTIN   I have to go. Time to move on.

ETHAN   What, you mean you're finished here?

MARTIN   Yeah.

ETHAN	But, what about your assignment?
DOUGLAS	Ethan, who the heck are you talking to over there?
ETHAN	Uh... nobody.
MARTIN	Nobody?
ETHAN	Well, not nobody.
DOUGLAS	Well, who then?
MARTIN	Yeah, who then?
ETHAN	Myself. I was just talking to myself. *(He takes the tray of hot chocolate to the living room area.)*
DOUGLAS	Well, you're makin' a fool out of yourself in front of this woman. She's going to think you're a flat out, certified...
	DOUGLAS freezes. TERESA freezes.
MARTIN	That's better. Nice fella, but awfully yappy, isn't he?
ETHAN	What happened?
MARTIN	I froze time.
ETHAN	What?
MARTIN	I froze time. I just learned it. Neat, huh?
ETHAN	You mean, time is frozen everywhere?
MARTIN	Everywhere.
ETHAN	France?

MARTIN	Frozen.
ETHAN	China?
MARTIN	Frozen.
ETHAN	Mexico?
MARTIN	Frozito.
ETHAN	Wow. What about me? Why aren't I frozen?
MARTIN	Because you're with me. *(He slaps ETHAN on the back.)*
ETHAN	Wait a minute. I felt that. You can touch me.
MARTIN	That's right. That's what I said. You're with me now.
ETHAN	But, you're dead.
MARTIN	Oh, sure. Keep throwing that in my face.
ETHAN	But, I'm not dead, am I?
MARTIN	No, no.
ETHAN	So, am I in the spirit world or are you in the real world?
MARTIN	Neither. We're on kind of a bridge that joins both worlds.
ETHAN	A bridge?
MARTIN	Yeah. Don't look down.

ETHAN, startled, looks down.

Listen, I've gotta run. *(moves right)*

ETHAN   Wait? You can't stay a bit longer?

MARTIN   Stay? Why would I want to stay? No, I'm anxious to get to where I'm going. See what it's like there. I hope it's warm. *(looking up)* Well... not too warm.

ETHAN   But, I thought it might be nice to spend a Christmas together.

MARTIN   No. No can do.

ETHAN   It's just one more day?

MARTIN   No. Besides, they're very strict. Once your assignment is completed, you've got to move on.

ETHAN   And you've completed yours?

MARTIN   Yeah.

ETHAN   What was it?

MARTIN   It was nothing. Not even worth talking about. So, anyway, that's it. Time to hit the road. It was nice seeing you again, brother.

ETHAN   Wait a minute. It was me, wasn't it? I was the assignment. I was the one you had to set on the right path.

MARTIN   No.

ETHAN   Sure it was. With the eggs, and Teresa and all that.

MARTIN   No, it wasn't you, Ethan.

ETHAN

Well, who was it?

MARTIN

It was me. I was my assignment. I had to set myself on the right path.

ETHAN

I don't understand.

MARTIN

Ethan, I'm sorry. I took something from you a long time ago that I shouldn't have.

ETHAN

What?

MARTIN

(Beat.) Me. Your brother. And the love that you should've had from your brother. I wasn't there for you. I let you down, Ethan, and I'm sorry. I don't expect sixty thousand eggs to make it right, but I've never been as creative as you, and it was the best I could come up with. Now, I've got to go. They don't like it if you don't come when you're called. *(He moves toward the door.)*

ETHAN

I'm never going to see you again?

MARTIN

No. But, that's okay. You're going to be just fine without me.

ETHAN

You think so?

MARTIN

(looks at TERESA and DOUGLAS) I know so. You know, Ethan, I learned something here this week. Dad was right. I guess I should've listened to him. Things might've been different between us.

The door swings open. MARTIN moves to it.

ETHAN

Martin?

	MARTIN stops. ETHAN moves to him and gives him a hug. MARTIN is surprised, and after a moment, hugs him back.
MARTIN	Yeah, well, I gotta go. Have a nice Christmas, Nancy, and uh... can I tell you one more thing?
ETHAN	What?
MARTIN	That is the ugliest Christmas tree I have ever seen. *(Beat.)* Goodbye, Ethan.
ETHAN	Goodbye, Martin.
	MARTIN moves outside. Suddenly the outside is brightly illuminated.
MARTIN	Oh, sure. Now with the light!
	The door closes. When it does, time unfreezes.
DOUGLAS	Lunatic! *(He realizes that ETHAN isn't where he was standing when they started this conversation.)* What the.... How'd you do that?
ETHAN	Do what?
DOUGLAS	That. You were just... I was... and now you're...
ETHAN	You must be tired, Douglas. Come over here and have some hot chocolate and then you can go home to your wife.
TERESA	What's this?
ETHAN	What?

> *TERESA moves out. She is carrying a*
> *small wrapped parcel.*

TERESA   This. I found it under the tree, but, I
don't think it was there a minute ago.
At least I didn't see it. Here, Ethan.
Open it.

> *TERESA hands the package to ETHAN.*

ETHAN   Why me?

TERESA   Well, it's got your name on it.

ETHAN   What?

TERESA   Yeah. See? *(She hands the gift to
ETHAN.)*

ETHAN   Did Caroline send me a gift, Douglas?

DOUGLAS   Well, if she did, she didn't mention it to
me.

TERESA   Open it.

> *ETHAN opens the gift. It is the painting of*
> *his mother.*

DOUGLAS   Well, look at that.

TERESA   Who is it?

ETHAN   It's... a portrait of my mother.

TERESA   Well, who could've sent that?

ETHAN   I think I have an idea.

DOUGLAS   Well, you know in my house, we have a
tradition. We always toast the opening
of the first Christmas gift. In fact, in my
house we toast the opening of every

gift. So, what do you say? (*He picks up his hot chocolate.*) Here's to the first gift of Christmas.

They all raise their glasses.

TERESA   And to good friends.

ETHAN   And to family.

They toast. A light shines down on ETHAN. He holds his glass up to the heavens. Lights down.

End.

After twenty-five-years in radio arts, Norm Foster discovered the world of theatre and began his legacy as Canada's most-produced playwright. He has penned an impressive array of plays, including a handful of musicals, that have been produced across North America. Norm lives in Ancaster, Ontario. Find out more at www.normfoster.com

RECYCLED
Paper made from
recycled material
FSC® C103567

Marquis Book Printing Inc.

Québec, Canada
2012

Printed on Silva Enviro 100% post-consumer EcoLogo certified paper,
processed chlorine free and manufactured using biogas energy.

100%   PERMANENT